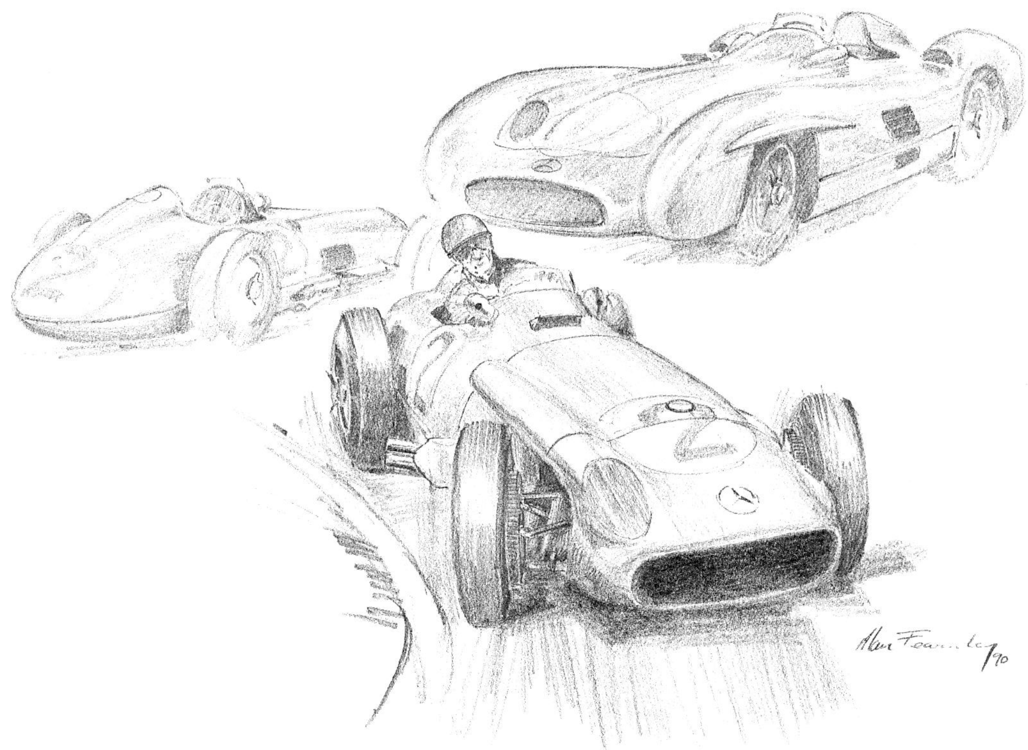

MERCEDES-BENZ

THE ART OF ALAN FEARNLEY

by

Eric Dymock

ISBN 0 - 9516780 - 0 - 0
Mercedes-Benz, the art of Alan Fearnley
British Library Cataloguing in Publication Data
Dymock, Eric
Mercedes-Benz : the art of Alan Fearnley,
1. English paintings, Fearnley, Alan, 1942-
1. Title II, Fearnley, Alan *1942-*
759.2

Published by Grand Prix Sportique
Upton, Tetbury, Glos, GL8 8LP

Produced by Dove Publishing, Sutton Veny, Wilts

November 1990

INTRODUCTION

from

Hans Tauscher

Managing Director Mercedes-Benz (United Kingdom) Limited

The first painting of Alan Fearnley's that I saw was his evocative re-creation of the 1914 Grand Prix at Lyon. Here was every quality a fine painting should encompass - an eye for detail, superb composition and a vivid portrayal of the action of the period.

Alan's skills are unique. He is a gifted landscape painter and yet he understands the world of motor racing like a true enthusiast. Much of his success derives from his talent for really studying his subject before commencing work, and this is evident in his completed paintings.

Recently Mercedes-Benz (United Kingdom) Limited commissioned three oil paintings depicting important moments in our racing history. They grace our offices and are a constant source of attention. I hope you enjoy Eric Dymock's perceptive analysis of Alan's Mercedes art as much as we enjoy our collection of his work.

ACKNOWLEDGEMENTS

This book celebrates the completion by Alan Fearnley of three commemorative paintings commissioned by Mercedes-Benz (United Kingdom) Ltd, depicting the 1914 French Grand Prix, the 1939 Tripoli Grand Prix, and the 1989 Grand Prix d'Endurance at Le Mans. It details the background to these events, captured on canvas in oils, in which Mercedes-Benz cars have scored some of their most notable victories. The originals of all three paintings hang in the Milton Keynes headquarters of Mercedes-Benz (United Kingdom) Ltd.

Alan Fearnley's work, commissioned by Grand Prix Sportique and its clients, includes other paintings featuring the racing cars of Mercedes-Benz. Together with the Mercedes-Benz owned paintings, "There's Only One Winner" and "The Argentine Grand Prix 1955" are available as limited edition prints from Grand Prix Sportique, the publishers of this book.

The two remaining works, "Monaco 1937" and "Donington 1989" are reproduced here by kind permission of their owners.

CONTENTS

ALAN FEARNLEY

When he was painting railway locomotives, Alan Fearnley could use clouds of steam and smoke to convey power and speed.

"It isn't so easy with cars," he says. "You have to manipulate shapes. The position of the car on the canvas is important. So is the profile of the clouds. Even the way the spectators are facing. You have to use line and perspective to supply movement - to guide the eye through the picture - make the eye race along to communicate quickness or acceleration."

For the teenage Alan Fearnley, colouring prints in a photographic studio, detailing and accuracy were crucial. He had to see past the photographer's lens, create images that a camera could not achieve. When he was not colouring-in portraits, he became an impressionist painter, using outlines and profiles and textured colours to persuade the eye it was seeing something it wasn't.

A patch of blue became a railway bridge with a curving arch, a thin pillar of brown a column of smoke from an industrial landscape in his own Yorkshire bailiewick.

"They were semi-abstract works, built up with dabs of colour, rather than in detail or with the realism of the captured moment."

But even the most abstract artists have to make a living, and Alan Fearnley earned his working for a greetings card manufacturer.

"I began to enjoy the technique. It was more demanding in some ways than doing impressionist paintings which require less skill in the act of painting. I turned towards a more illustrative style. My subject matter changed away from landscapes and topography towards transport. Next to cars I loved railway engines and there were more of them in Ilkley and West Yorks than there were racing cars, so I painted them."

Alan Fearnley's evocative locomotives and moody engine sheds became famous. The founder chairman of the Guild of Railway Artists, he published a large portfolio, magnificent canvasses in oil and acrylics, as notable for their atmosphere and landscape quality as their technical rectitude.

Painting motor racing was not a departure for Alan Fearnley. Among his non-railway work were paintings of ships, aircraft, even a nuclear power station and scenes of military battles. Racing cars were a first love however, and following some important commissions, he turned to them with enthusiasm.

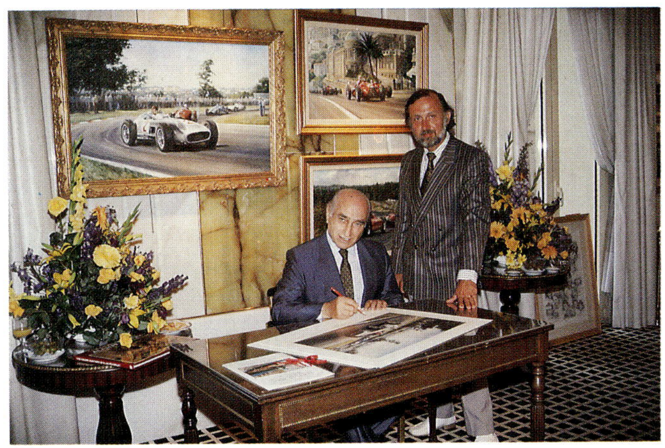

"I sometimes produce detailed drawings on tracing paper in order to achieve the right relationships within a painting. Just occasionally, when the main area is made up of landscape, I may suggest the composition on the canvas with a few pencil lines or brush strokes."

Fearnley confesses that he does allow some "flexibility" concerning strict accuracy in his paintings.

"I believe that interpretation is more important than the subject, and while the racing cars themselves have to be treated with the utmost accuracy, the laws of artistic licence can be applied to everything else. I am quite happy to correct a landscape by adding or subtracting trees, or animating onlookers to make a point."

One of the problems facing a work such as a painting of a racing car is for it to be taken seriously by the art world. It is a common problem with what Fearnley calls the enthusiast school of painting which includes railway, aviation, or motoring art.

"Sometimes pictures of this sort appeal only to railway, aeroplane, or car enthusiasts, and critics and the art establishment ignore them. It doesn't seem to apply to marine paintings, because that is a longer established and better recognised school, and in any case is preoccupied with the elements of the sky and the weather and the sea."

Fearnley is now convinced that if the enthusiast school is ever to be recognised and valued as it ought to be, it must produce pictures of such an artistic quality that they can be appreciated and valued by art lovers. They must also have pictorial merit to hang anywhere, not only in the study of a car enthusiast.

His rise to the challenge of Mercedes-Benz, in producing works of art is celebrated in this book.

"I enjoyed all of the pictures for different reasons. The 1914 Grand Prix was romantic, with the curve of the track leading the eye through the car into the unknown. I had to try and invoke the heat of competition and the dust and flying stones as the road broke up in the summer sunshine. I love painting that era of motor racing. There is a famous photograph of that corner, but I have moved the perspective and taken a few small liberties with some aspects of the scenery."

Tripoli made different demands.

"I had to show the heat, the drama of the moment when Lang had outflanked Caracciola, the confusion of the start. I chose a viewpoint where no camera could ever be; I use photographic references but only for guidance. It was a moment in motor racing history that had been inadequately recorded; a great opportunity to capture the excitement of an instant against a background of triumphalist Italian architecture."

Le Mans has colour, movement, and a modern vigour of its own. "I miss painting the drivers in open cars. You can convey so much if you can see their arms or even their face, but I managed to make up for this with the flag marshals in the Le Mans painting. There is so much to work with in figures."

Fearnley completed three paintings in oils for Mercedes-Benz (Great Britain) Ltd, commemorating the 1914, 1939, and 1989 races. They were made available in a series of limited edition prints, and the originals were secured for display in the headquarters building in Milton Keynes. Four other commissions featuring Mercedes-Benz racing cars are illustrated in this book together with a number of remarques, accompanying sketches, which illustrate the graphic style of an accomplished artist in a demanding medium.

TEAM CONQUEST: THE 1914 FRENCH GRAND PRIX

Motor racing was already ten years old when the French coined *"Grand Prix"* for a new competition which would signify the start of a new era. The great city to city races were no more. The carnage of the 1903 Paris-Madrid, stopped at Bordeaux because of accidents, had seen to that. The international team events of the Gordon Bennett generation were also all but gone.

The new title was for racing on a closed circuit between cars rather than between nations. Cars and drivers would henceforth compete individually for prize money, there would be accolades for winning makes, and for drivers money and adulation that would turn them into folk heroes.

The change took a little time, and even the French journal *L'Auto* was uncertain what the incentive was.

"Ah, oui, la Grande Epreuve est la passionnante preuve que ce Grand Prix de l'Automobile Club de France, grande bataille industrielle de l'automobile".

Yet large prize money distinguished Grands Prix from other races only for as long as the French kept the title to themselves. As the great competitions proliferated, they evolved into the *"Gran Premio"* and the *"Grosser Preis"* throughout the continent of Europe.

The organisers' lofty ideals were not invariably sustained however, and the regulations were often ill-conceived, at the whim of a local grandee or a well-meaning committee, uncertain whether they were encouraging the development of automobilism or merely putting on a spectacular event.

The early rules involved complicated formulae taking account of weight and fuel consumption

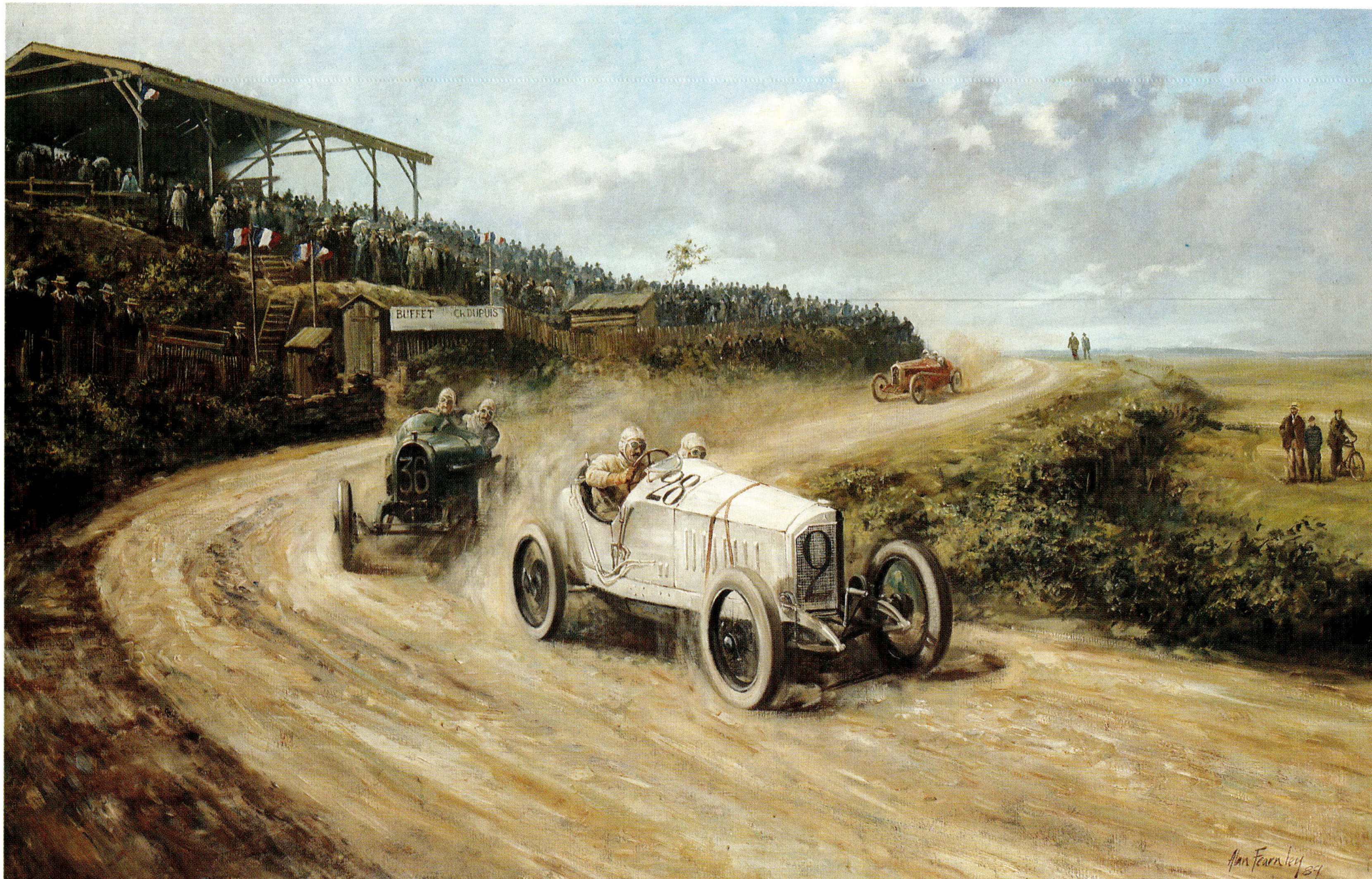
BUFFET
Ch. DUPUIS
Alan Fearnley 84

until, in some desperation, an easily verifiable standard for competing cars was worked out. For the French Grand Prix of 1914, the engine swept volume was fixed at 4.5 litres, and the cars limited to 1,100kg (2425lb, 21.65cwt).

The Automobile Club de France chose a new twenty-three mile course near Lyon because the local authority made it an offer it could not afford to refuse, and the stage was set for one of the most famous races of all time.

The international scene was a sombre one. The race was scheduled for July 4th 1914, a bare six days after the fatal shots that began the Great War, had been fired at Sarajevo. The assassination of the Archduke Franz Ferdinand, "shook the conscience of the world", said The Times.

Despite the high feelings in France and Germany however, the race had long been arranged and on it went. A field of thirty-seven cars from five nations assembled, technically the most distinguished ever. All except the sleeve-valve Piccart-Pictets had the new overhead camshaft engines. Delage, Nagant, Sunbeam, and Vauxhall had twin overhead camshafts, and nearly every engine now had four valves per cylinder.

Outputs of 120 horse power were not uncommon, and the Vauxhall engines were reputed to reach 4,000 rpm. Delage, Fiat, and Peugeot had four wheel brakes. Mercedes chose their customary measured approach, with technicians and drivers visiting the track in the spring, to ensure that the cars would be well-matched to the terrain.

Paul Daimler was Mercedes' chief engineer, and although the car he designed for the 1914 French Grand Prix was not the most advanced in the field, it had been well conceived. Its four cylinder engine was derived from the Mercedes aero engine, the cylinders were made from individual steel forgings with a welded-on water jacket, enabling it to be made from thin metal which kept the weight down and ensured even cooling.

Daimler's creation provided 115 horse power, giving the cars a top speed of over 100mph when they left the factory. By the time they were in race tune, they could do 120mph. There was the customary Mercedes attention to detail. The rear axle contained double pinions and crown wheels machined integrally with the half-shafts, which were hollowed-out to save weight.

The axle itself was a masterpiece of precision, for which twenty-four gears making up six sets of ratios were machined beforehand. These gave the drivers a choice of ratios, from 2.2 down to 2.8:1, so

◀ *The 1914 Grand Prix at Lyon. Christian Lautenschlager driving his 4.5 litre Mercedes followed by Kenelm Lee Guinness in his Sunbeam*

that they could decide which was best for the undulating demanding track with its 100 corners. The gearing had to take account of a difference of 700 feet between the highest and lowest points on the course, and one leg was an eleven- mile switchback straight.

An entire generation of racing cars would pass before alternative gear ratios to suit drivers' tastes and different circuits would become commonplace. Pre-race preparation on this level would become a custom that the Mercedes racing department would follow for the next seventy-five years.

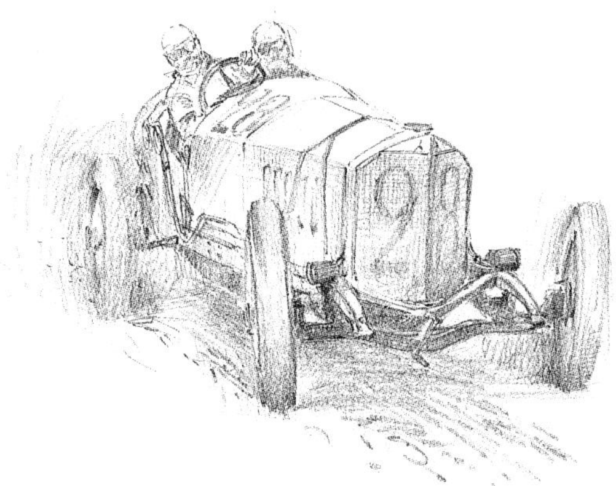

Five cars, the most permitted under the regulations, was a large team, but everything about this Mercedes endeavour was thorough. Nothing was left to chance. A contemporary writer noted that

"...everything was orderly, almost military, and on a big scale. There appeared to be enough spare parts to put together a couple of engines."

At first it looked as though the Delage and Peugeot drivers might not arrive back from racing at Indianapolis in time for practice. The team managers were confident, but star drivers were important ingredients for success on such a tricky circuit. In the nick of time the local authorities relented, extra practice periods were allowed, and the French regained the initiative.

The crowd was around 300,000, although the real number will never be known.

"Every seat in the grandstand was occupied. The hillside opposite seemed black with people, and so great was the press of cars on the road that many who thought two hours sufficient to cover the 12 miles separating Lyons and the start of the race, were doomed to arrive after most of the competitors had started."

The cars were sent off in pairs at 30-second intervals, starting at 08.00. Nazzaro in a car of his own design, and the French hero and winner of the 1913 race George Boillot (Peugeot) both jumped the start. So did Christian Lautenschlager and Otto Salzer (Mercedes). It was a tense moment. Louis Wagner (Mercedes) and Salzer were stopped by a marshal as a penalty, Salzer's stop oiling his plugs which further delayed him.

All thirty-seven cars started, twenty remorseless laps lay ahead, and to the delight of the crowd, Boillot was first to get round the 23.38 mile (37.63 km) lap back to the pits and grandstands at the Sept Chemins hairpin on Route Nationale 86. But Max Sailer, who had started two minutes behind Boillot, had closed up. It was the Mercedes, not the Peugeot, which really led the race on the big scoreboard. By lap 3 Sailer was 1 min 37 sec ahead, and Jules Goux had lost fifth place to Lautenschlager.

By five laps the Mercedes had overtaken Boillot, and Sailer, after setting fastest lap in 20 min 06 sec; an average speed of 69.8 mph (112.3 kph), built up a lead of almost three minutes. Yet the pace was too furious for his luck to hold, and after two hours' racing, a connecting rod failed and the car clattered to a stop by the side of the road.

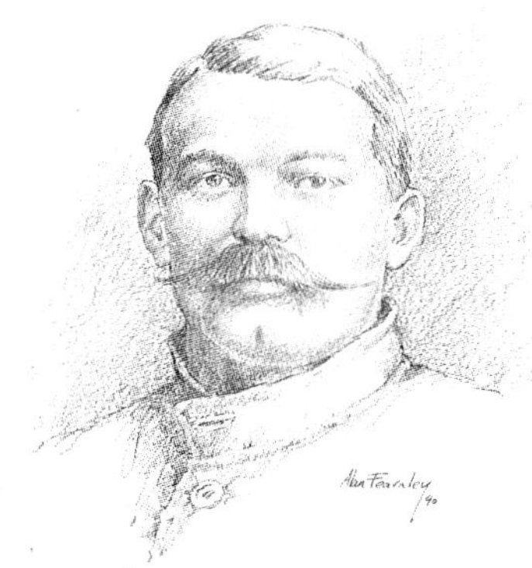

The object of Sailer's sprint had been to stretch Boillot's Peugeot to the limit. When Sailer retired, Lautenschlager was only a minute behind Boillot, watching and waiting for the French car to falter in the four hours' racing which still lay ahead.

After Lautenschlager stopped to change tyres, Boillot's lead stretched to four minutes, but his car had lost its edge. The tempo of those hectic opening laps had been so fast that the Delages, the Vauxhalls, the Fiats, and two of the Sunbeams were left smoking by the roadside. Only the Peugeots and the Mercedes remained in the running.

On lap 11, just after half distance, Wagner moved up to third behind Lautenschlager, while the second Peugeot, driven by Goux, was overhauled remorselessly by Salzer in the third surviving Mercedes. Boillot drove the race of his life.

"He took his turns as never before; changed tyres in amazing time; he pushed his motor to the limit on the switchback straight."

Lautenschlager attacked on lap 16 of the 20 lap race, cutting the gap to 2 min 05 sec. On the next lap it was a bare 14 sec. On lap 18 he was half a minute ahead, on lap 19 more than a minute. He had paced himself perfectly. Boillot's car stammered gamely on with one cylinder out of action, and Salzer took fourth place from the gallant Goux.

Boillot's race ended on the same section of the course as his early adversary, Sailer. The Peugeot's number 3 exhaust valve had failed, and the engine was destroyed. His weak front brakes had given out and his rear drums were blue and distorted with the heat. Boillot, stopped by the roadside, saw for the first time in the course of the gruelling seven hours, the Mercedes of Christian Lautenschlager as it swept past to victory.

Alan Fearnley's painting portrays Lautenschlager's car rounding the Piège de la Mort which followed the long and punishing straight close to the end of the lap, ahead of Kenelm Lee Guiness's Sunbeam. Guinness retired on lap 9 with engine trouble but another Sunbeam, driven by Dario Resta, finished fifth behind the three Mercedes and Goux's Peugeot.

Twenty years later, SCH Davis, sports editor of *The Autocar* who watched the 1914 Grand Prix, wrote

"There was something more than motor racing in the atmosphere as the crowds made their way dustily from the course. Never before has there been that curiously indefinable feeling and everyone was extraordinarily quiet. Had the gift of foresight been ours, what, I wonder, would one have thought; as it was there was quite distinctly the feeling that a menacing though invisible presence had been manifest. The thing disappeared in an hour or two, normality returned; but though we knew nothing of it, there had come faintly on the wind the echoing thud of guns."

The next time the Mercedes engine was seen, it was in a German fighting aeroplane. The old order in Europe was swept away by a war in which Boillot was one of the casualties, shot down over the Western Front in 1916.

The 1914 French Grand Prix was the last won by a car with brakes on two wheels only, but the GP Mercedes went on racing. In 1915 it won the Indianapolis 500 miles at an average speed of 89.84 mph which remained unbeaten for several years. In 1922 it won the Targa Florio in Sicily with front brakes added, then with a supercharger won its last race as a works entry in 1926.

KING OF TRIPOLI: THE 1939 TRIPOLI GRAND PRIX

The most significant race of 1939 was not one of the major *Grandes Epreuves,* the national Grand Prix races counting towards the European championship. Instead, on the far side of the Mediterranean, a minor event was given celebrity treatment and an unaccustomed budget with the aim of enhancing Italian prestige in Libya.

Across Mussolini's *Mare Nostrum*, in a new outpost of the Italian Empire, the Tripoli Grand Prix was promoted on a lavish scale as a means of impressing the natives with Italian wealth and vigour. The 8.14 mile (13.09 km) Mellaha circuit was one of the best and fastest in the world.

Mellaha, between Tripoli and the small town of Tagiura, was opened in 1925, and first found a place in motor racing history with a celebrated scandal. In 1933 it was the scene of the only known occasion when the drivers fixed the result of a Grand Prix.

The Italian authorities sold some four million tickets for a state lottery on the results of the 1933 Tripoli Grand Prix. The winner stood to gain some 50,000 lire - a good deal of money in the depressed early 1930s.

Thirty winning tickets corresponded to the thirty starters, the jackpot going to whoever held the number of the winning driver. The individual who had drawn Achille Varzi saw an opportunity to ensure his luck held, and proposed a share of the winnings if only Varzi would arrange the result. Varzi's rivals accordingly dropped out in the course of the race, Nuvolari's car expiring mysteriously just short of the line while leading, but managing to re-start just as Varzi took the chequered flag.

The calumny was covered up, and the rules were changed to prevent it ever happening again, but the Grand Prix went on. From 1935, the Germans won every time; Auto Union and Mercedes-Benz

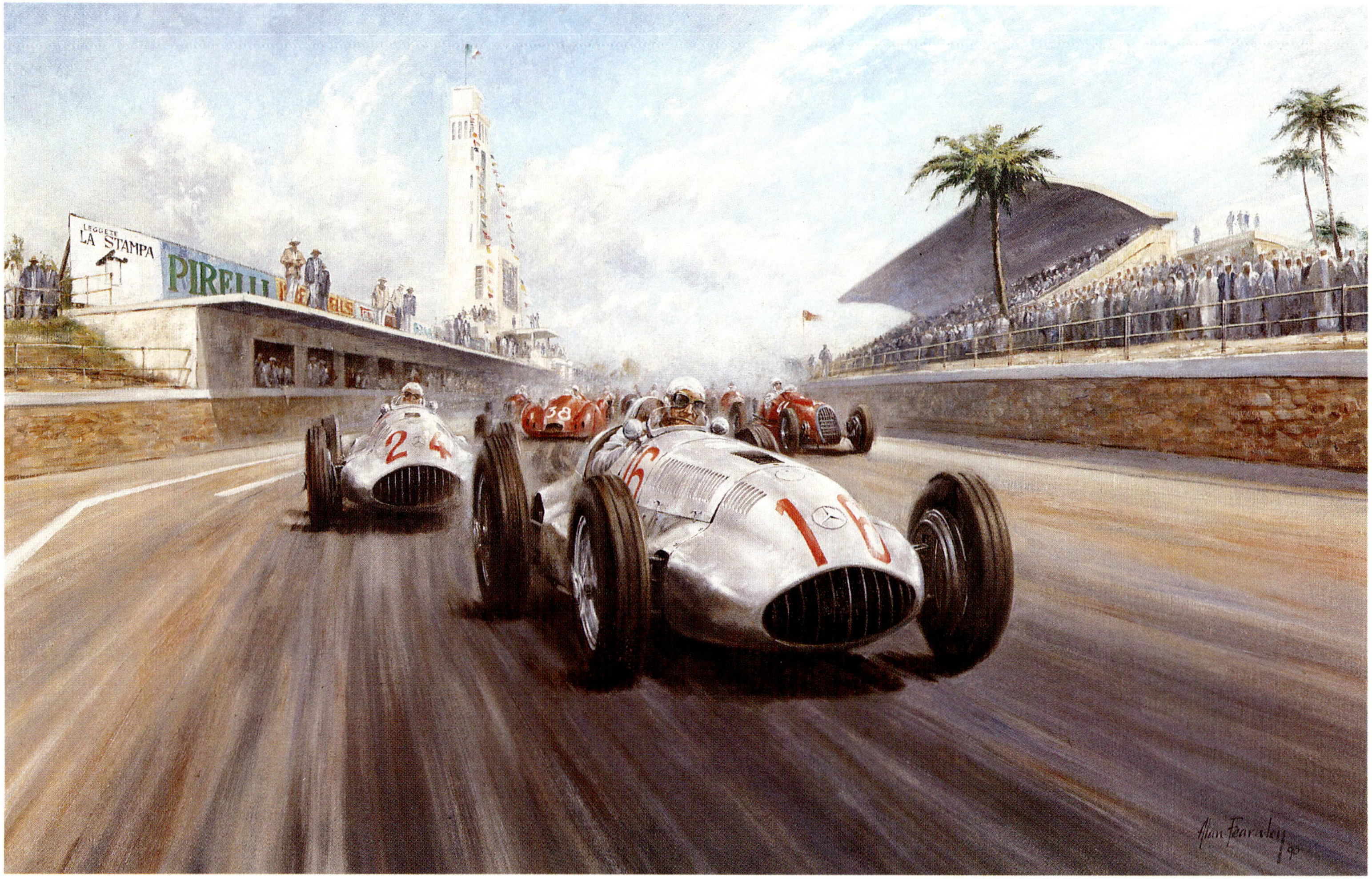
LEGGETE
LA STAMPA
PIRELLI
Alan Fearnley
'90

between them taking the first three places, and Hermann Lang winning in 1937 and 1938.

For 1939, the Italians had a plan. Weary of being overpowered by Mercedes-Benz and Auto Union in Grand Prix racing, the state-owned car company, Alfa Romeo, turned instead to motor racing's second division, voiturette racing. It had been going almost as long as the premier division, which was run for 850 kg (1874 lb) cars with 3 litre supercharged and 4.5 litre unsupercharged engines.

Voiturettes went back to Edwardian times, when the engine limit was 3 litres, but in the impoverished post-war world it had emerged as a largely amateur category for cars of 1,100 cc or 1.5 litres. The races were mostly shorter and less demanding.

By the 1930s, voiturettes had a programme of racing to themselves, with Bugattis and Maseratis competing vigorously with ERAs. It even created its own heroes such as the daring Richard Seaman in his beautifully-presented ten year old black Delage. His performances earned him a seat in the Mercedes-Benz Grand Prix team, in which he drove with great distinction until his tragic death, the only fatality in a Mercedes-Benz Grand Prix car, in 1939.

Voiturette racing had become so important and that prescient Alfa Romeo team manager, Enzo Ferrari challenged Gioacchino Colombo to devise a 1.5 litre supercharged car for it. He was convinced that when the international authorities proposed new rules for Grand Prix racing in 1941, they would take the voiturette formula, and make it the Formula A as it was known, for subsequent years.

Colombo drew up one of the greatest racing cars ever. The Alfa Romeo 158 (15 for 1.5 litre, 8 for eight cylinders) was a masterpiece of precision, with a tubular frame, a pointed tail, and an elegance that made it look a match for anything. The Alfettas, as they became known, finished first and second in their first race, the Coppa Ciano Junior at Leghorn, and the stage was set for an historic decision.

The Italian Automobile Federation was confident that the Alfetta even in its first modest form with 190 horse power together with the promising new 16-valve Maserati 4CL, were capable of beating anything in voiturette racing. So, for 1939, it issued a decree that all races on Italian soil would henceforth be for 1.5 litre cars. And Italian soil included Tripolitania, where the prestige event was scheduled for May.

◀ Hermann Lang and Rudolf Caracciola (Mercedes-Benz W165) in the 1939 Tripoli Grand Prix

Compared with European tracks, Mellaha was extravagantly furnished, with a permanent grandstand in gleaming white concrete and a tall white timing tower. Dick Seaman called it "an Ascot of motor racing". There was an adjoining hotel, the Uaddan with a casino and a theatre, and superbly laid-out pits. The prize-fund was generous - no more cheating was allowed - and there was lavish hospitality.

Yet Mercedes-Benz and Auto Union were just as capable as Enzo Ferrari at interpreting straws in the wind. Small eight and twelve cylinder engines of watchmaking precision were already on their drawing boards. Secretly in Stuttgart, the W165, a scaled-down version of the car that was sweeping the board in Grand Prix racing, was taking shape.

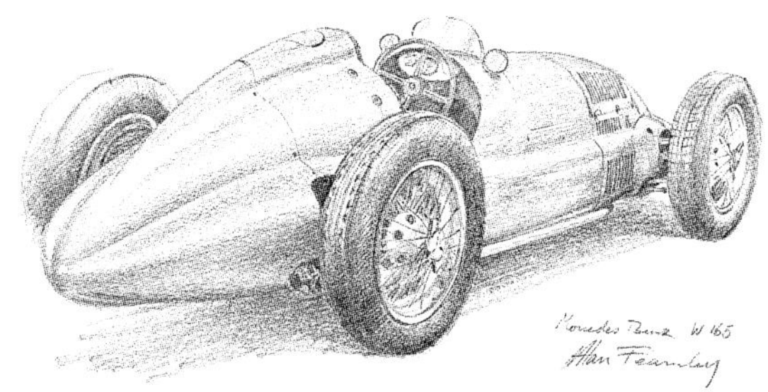

The W165 was as perfectly proportioned as the Alfa Romeo, with a two-stage supercharged V-8 engine producing 260 bhp at 8,500 rpm. Further supercharging the little engine later generated 278 bhp at 8,250 rpm.

The W165 was completed in the astonishingly short time of eight weeks; one of the cars was only finished by Mercedes' mechanics on the boat in which it was shipped across the Mediterranean.

Uncharacteristically, the atmosphere in the Mercedes team was unharmonious. During the second day's practice, Villoresi's new streamlined Maserati set fastest time ahead of Lang and Caracciola. Alfred Neubauer, Mercedes' renowned team manager, had elected not to take part in the day's practice, but when Villoresi posted the time that would put him at the front of the grid, he sent his two drivers out on the sun-baked track to try and improve on it.

Caracciola was worried by Lang, a former racing mechanic eight years his junior. As senior driver, he expected Lang to know his place. But on the hot track, it was Lang who was faster, and Caracciola who had been the swiftest driver of his day was disconsolate. Neither could match Villoresi, but Caracciola sulked, and complained that Lang's car had been faster.

The drivers argued over gear ratios, but the Mercedes racing director, Max Sailer, the man who had goaded Boillot into blowing his engine up in the 1914 French Grand Prix, knew racing drivers. He ordered that Caracciola should have the choice of car and gear

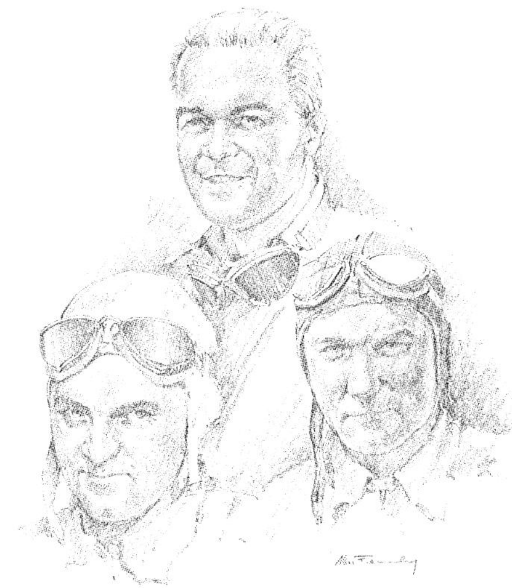

ratios. Carraciola chose the car with the better acceleration, and it was Lang's turn to sulk.

When Marshal Balbo, the Governor of Libya dropped the starter's flag, the two Mercedes-Benzes faced a formidable array of Maseratis, of which three were works 4CLs for Count Trossi, Luigi Villoresi, and Franco Cortese, and six Alfa Romeos.

The Mercedes-Benz tactics were for Lang to go flat-out, even if it meant a pit stop to change tyres, just as Sailer had done in 1914, and tempt the opposition to over-rev engines, wear out brakes, and ultimately fail. Caracciola was expected to conserve his energies, run steadily, and win.

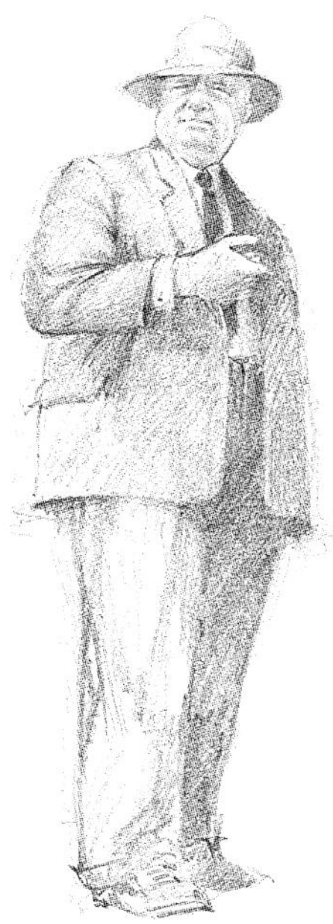

But as the cars lined up on the grid, Villoresi in pole position, Lang alongside him, then Caracciola, Lang noticed a starting light on the gantry over the pits. He asked Neubauer if he should watch the light or Marshal Balbo's flag.

The team chief consulted race officials, who said the light signalled the official start, and in the event the Marshal's arm was a fraction late. Lang siezed his opportunity. Off he went ahead of the flag-watchers, and none of them ever saw him again.

Only Farina was able to challenge Lang and he even led Caracciola briefly. The Alfas wilted in the blazing heat. The team's sole survivor, Emilio Villoresi limping in nearly eight minutes in arrears. None of the works Maseratis lasted so much as a lap - the Italians' humiliation was complete.

Caracciola was angry at what he regarded almost as cheating. The mischievous Lang was unrepentant, and won at 122.91 mph only a fraction slower than Caracciola's speed in the large powerful W 25 four years earlier. Lang's fastest lap was 133.5 mph against Villoresi's 134 mph in practice with the streamlined Maserati.

The W 165 never raced again. Dick Seaman drove one at the Nürburgring and described it in a letter to the Mercedes-Benz historian George Monkhouse.

"It is very small and light to handle, but definitely goes, especially around slow corners. It is extremely easy to drive."

He tried to get the racing department to enter one for the 1939 Nuffield trophy at Donington in June, but nothing came of it.

Alan Fearnley has caught the triumph in Lang's face as he races ahead of Caracciola into the left handed bend after the pits. Behind him is the red streamlined Maserati of Villoresi, and over on the right, the 158 Alfa Romeo, not yet in its better-known form with the broad grille with which it raced in the 1940s and 1950s.

Hermann Lang had a long and distinguished motor racing career which began on motorcycles in 1928 and went on until he came second in the gruelling Carrera Panamericana, and won Le Mans with Fritz Reiss in the 300SL in 1952. The only pre-war Mercedes works driver to make a successful comeback after the war, his final race was the German Grand Prix of 1954 when, lying in second place behind Fangio in another W 196 Mercedes-Benz, he spun off while racing his team-mate Karl Kling. Lang worked with Mercedes-Benz until 1974 and died in 1987.

Rudolf Caracciola, a great natural driver, remained with Mercedes-Benz throughout most of a brilliant career which ended at much the same time as Lang's but less happily. After finishing fourth in the 1952 Mille Miglia, he crashed in a sports car race at Berne, sustaining injuries from which he never fully recovered. Caracciola died in 1959.

The W165s were never allowed to develop as the Alfas' adversaries; the world was denied a resolution of the conflict. Instead they were preserved for posterity much as they were when they took the chequered flag on the historic day at Tripoli, ending an era of motor racing, the like of which was never seen again.

SILVER ARROWS: LE MANS 1989

A motor race that is something between the Grand National and the World Cup in its spectacle and universal reputation, the *Grand Prix d'Endurance* is unique in motoring sport. Rivalled in prestige, if not in riches, only by the Indianapolis 500, Le Mans is a hallmark of motor sporting achievement. Winning makes all the difference between a make of car achieving classic status and being remembered only as a make of car.

Ferrari, Porsche, Bentley, Bugatti, Alfa Romeo, Aston Martin, Jaguar, Mercedes-Benz - the winners' names read like a roll-call of the greatest and best in motoring. There have been interlopers. Ford challenged the world and won four years in a row. Alpine-Renault won for France, and so did the missile firm, Matra.

It took Renault years of costly effort. In 1977, having vowed to carry on until they won, the team suffered the humiliation of having all their cars blow up spectacularly and publicly on the Mulsanne Straight. There was no chance of fudging an excuse; dense clouds of smoke from engines destroying themselves in front of a world audience could not be explained away as anything but a catastrophe.

Le Mans is unique. Round-the-clock racing takes place elsewhere, but nowhere has the history, the ambience, the tradition of racing at night and in the morning, racing bleary-eyed and continuous, racing as a way of life for twenty-four crowded hours. Twenty-four hours packed with drama and incident in one of the world's major sporting events that has proved an elusive prize for many a well-motivated and well-funded and highly skilled team of great cars.

It was not easy for Mercedes-Benz to return to Le Mans. No obloquy was ever attached to the car

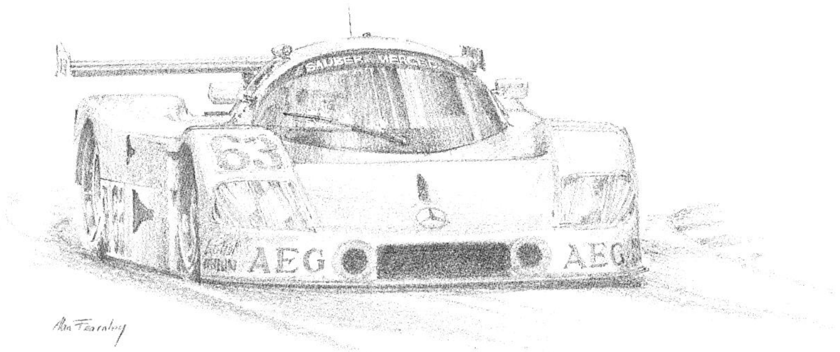

in the disaster of 1955, but it was a sensitive issue. Now, in 1989 they were back, Silver Arrows once again, doing 230 mph along the murderous three mile Mulsanne straight, the longest in motor racing.

It took over a minute to get from one end to the other, so the drivers spent some six hours out of the twenty-four travelling on land faster than many commercial aircraft fly.

Carefully designed aerodynamics, acting in the opposite sense to an aircraft wing, help keep the car on the road. At these speeds taking-off is an ever-present danger, and the guard-rails along Mulsanne were made taller year by year.

Mercedes-Benz nearly won in 1930, against the smallest field in the history of the race. Rudolf Carraciola and Christian Werner challenged the mastery of the Bentleys with a 7.1 SS Mercedes-Benz, an impressive large white car against the green Speed Sixes and two blown 4.5 litres. A lone Mercedes against experienced adversaries.

Caracciola led from the start but the Mercedes pit work was slow and after handing over to Werner, the car's lead was only 1 min 49 sec over the fastest Bentley of Woolf Barnato and Glen Kidston. Barnato took the lead at 8.30 in the evening, lost it, regained it, and lost it again when the Bentley stopped for fuel.

The victory of the Sauber-Mercedes team, finishing first, second and fifth iin the 57th Le Mans 24 hour race on 10-11 June 1989. The winning car number 63 driven by Jochen Mass, Manuel Reuter and Stanley Dickens ▶

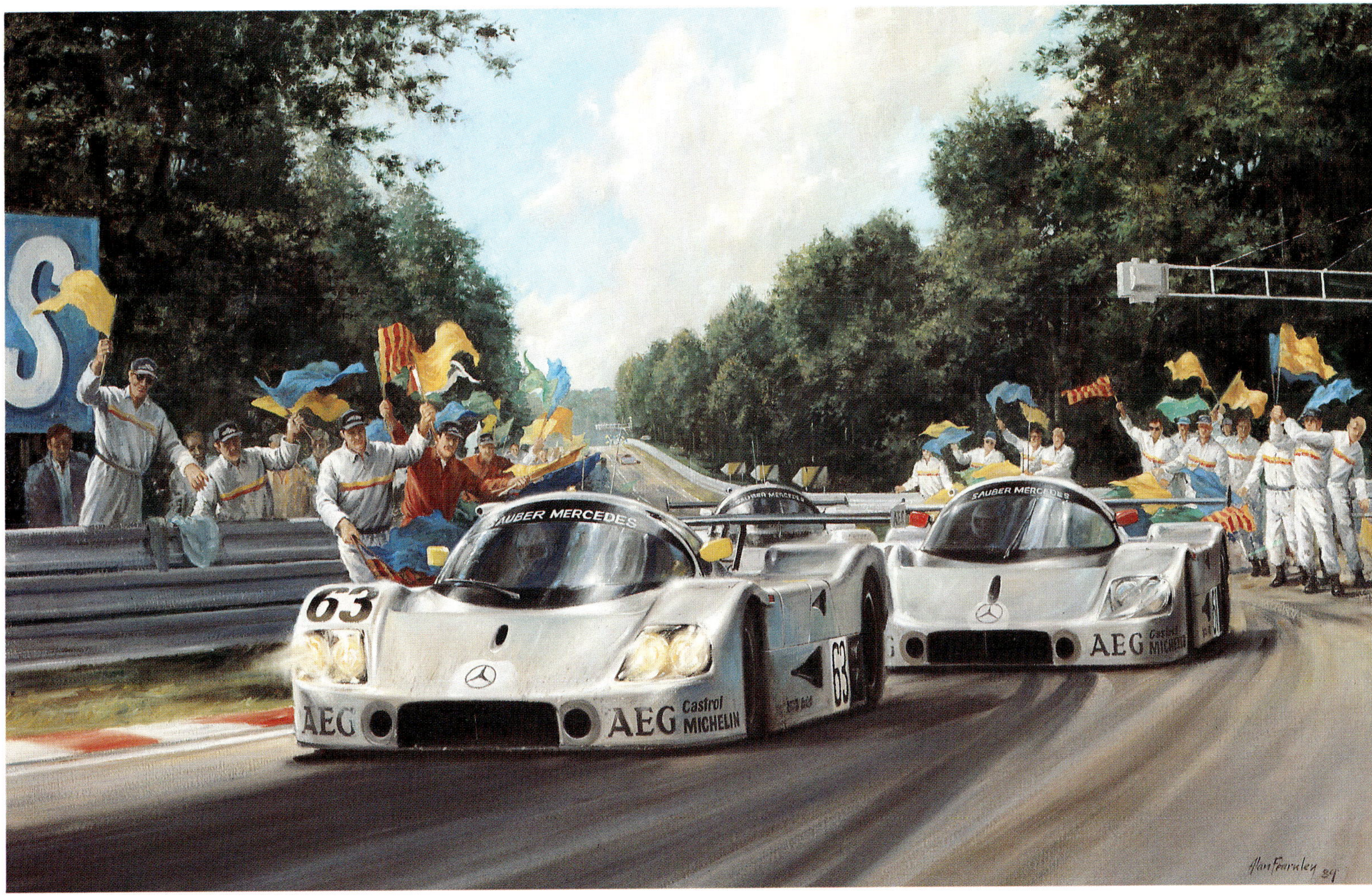
SAUBER MERCEDES
63
AEG
AEG
Castrol
MICHELIN
SAUBER MERCEDES
AEG
Castrol
MICHELIN
Alan Fearnley 89

After a seven minute pit stop at midnight, Caracciola took up the pursuit. Once again the lead was exchanged between the Bentley and the Mercedes. It was not until the small hours that the white car gave up. At 2.30 am it failed to restart after a pit stop - Neubauer said the dynamo had failed, and it was out, leaving victory to *"Old No 1"* which drove into history as the only car ever to have won the great race twice.

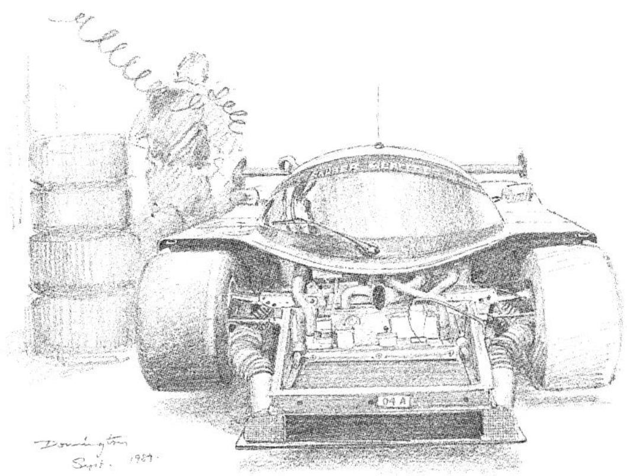

Mercedes came second in 1931, the first year of the Alfa Romeo domination of the race. A 7.1 litre SSK driven by Ivanowski and Stoffel covered 1,805 miles, but it was to be twenty-one years before the three-pointed star was once again in serious contention at the Circuit de la Sarthe.

The performance of the tubular-chassis 300SL, with its gull-wing doors made necessary to clear the high body sills, in the Mille Miglia of May 1952, showed it was faster than the Jaguars and Ferraris. It was also at least as good in handling and roadholding, and the threat it posed meant hasty changes to the Jaguar XK120C which had won the year before.

Jaguar redesigned their cooling system with a lower bonnet line to meet the challenge. It was an uncharacteristic mistake, and the cars failed through overheating. Le Mans is an unforgiving track.

Yet the 1952 victory was no walkover for the 300SL. The huge Cunninghams were fast and at midnight a Gordini led. Fog in the night slowed the pace of the race. The Gordini went out with brake failure and Pierre Levegh's big Talbot inherited the lead.

The two Mercedes ran consistently, four laps behind at one point, but in second and third places all they could do was run a well-organised and consistent race behind the large French car. Then, with only an hour and a quarter of the race left, a connecting rod in the Talbot's engine broke and Levegh was out.

Hermann Lang and Karl Reiss took the flag, followed by Fritz Helfrich and Karl Niedermayer. The winning car covered 2,320 miles at an average speed of 96.97 mph. It was not yet time for a 100 mph Le Mans; that distinction went to APR Rolt and Duncan

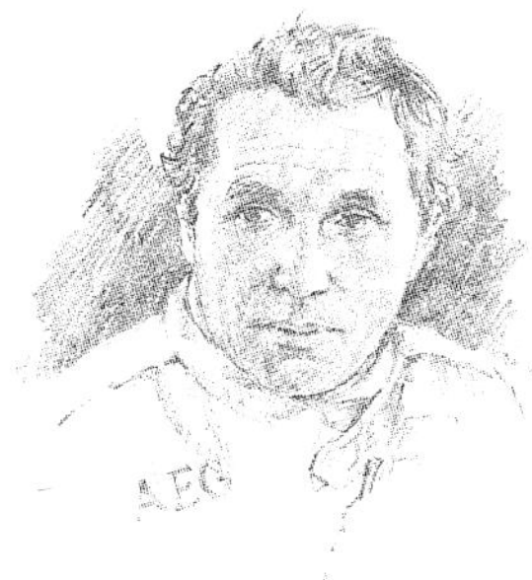

Hamilton, when they won in the new C-Type Jaguar in 1953.

In 1955, the directors in Stuttgart withdrew the cars after the accident. Levegh, the Frenchman who drove single-handedly against Mercedes-Benz in 1952 was included in the team of air-braked 300SLRs as a tribute to his gallantry. He it was alas, who was at the wheel when the awful chain of events began which led to the worst disaster in the history of motor racing.

The Circuit Permanent de la Sarthe, to the East of the Medieval town of Le Mans in the dusty western plain of France, remains a motor racing Mecca. The crowds are perhaps smaller now than the half-million or so who used to pack round the 8.4 mile track, camping in the pine woods, cramming the bars and restaurants, thronging the funfairs and amusement arcades. Now it is a TV spectacular, beamed with its successes - and failures - to an audience worldwide.

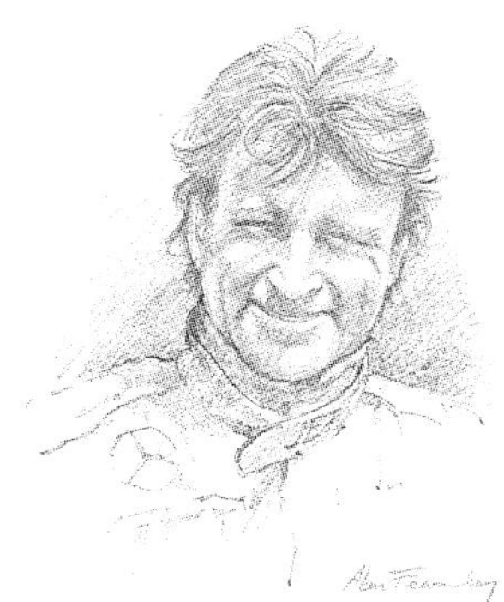

The 57th Vingt-Quatre Heures du Mans on June 10th and 11th, 1989, was a straight confrontation between Jaguar, winners in 1988, and Mercedes-Benz, whose team of Sauber Mercedes C9-88s had challenged Jaguar throughout the season. The field of fifty-five cars was probably the most testing in the history of the race, and on the Wednesday practice session, the Mercedes-Benz team gave notice that they were after outright victory.

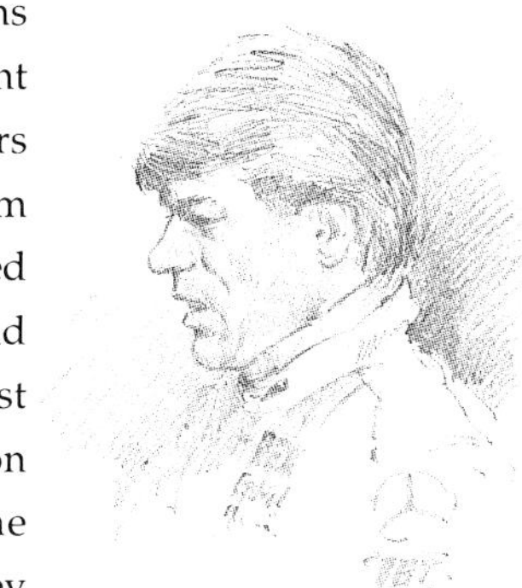

Just before the track was flooded by a sudden thunderstorm, Jean-Louis Schlesser did a fast qualifying lap during which he went through the timing trap on Mulsanne at exactly 250 mph. The Jaguars all improved on their previous year's speeds, but the fastest on Mulsanne was a clear 10 mph slower than the Mercedes. Schlesser went out towards the end of the qualifying sessions, and knocked half a second off his best lap to secure pole position on the starting grid.

Behind the Jaguars on the second row was Hans Stuck's Joest Porsche, behind that another Jaguar, then more Porsches. It was a glittering array of the finest and the fastest cars in long-distance endurance racing.

The pessimists regarded the Silver Arrows as fast but fragile. They were looked upon as essentially sprint cars that would not last the searing speed of the Mulsanne, together with the constant braking and gear changing and cornering during two full rounds of the clock against the experienced, battle-hardened crews from Jaguar and Porsche.

The Mercedes suffered gearbox failures during practice. Memories of 1988's mysterious tyre failures which had led to the cars' withdrawal were still fresh. Yet once the race began the team quickly established command. The winning car was not the hare at which the hounds had been baying. As in 1914 at Lyon, and 1939 at Tripoli, the fierce pace set in the opening laps left the opposition in disarray.

Driven by Jochen Mass, Manuel Reuter and Stanley Dickens, the winning car came from the sixth row of the grid, where it had been seven seconds slower than the other team cars of Jean-Louis Schlesser/Jean-Pierre Jabouille/Alain Cudini, and Mauro Baldi/Kenny Acheson/Gianfranco Brancatelli.

Mass battled with his old adversary, Hans Stuck's Porsche in the opening stages, taking the car up to second place. When Reuter took over, three laps were lost repairing damage when it struck debris on the track, dropping to 20th place.

It took until the 16th hour to regain the lead, but after that car 63 held its place until the end. The Mercedes staying power saw off its rivals and the cars finished first, second, and fifth. The best Porsche was third, the faster of the two surviving Jaguars fourth. Two Mazdas made it into the first ten, but the other factory teams from Aston Martin, Nissan, and Toyota were not in serious contention.

Winning Le Mans is a moment for any team to relish, and it is every team manager's ambition to demonstrate his command of the situation. At Le Mans, the traditional way to do so is to have sufficient time in hand to stage-manage a triumphant formation finish, with all the teams cars running together.

Alan Fearnley's painting depicts the Sauber-Mercedes cars on their lap of honour, on the right hand turn at the end of the Mulsanne straight. Here, where so many Le Mans hopes have been buried in the sand banks, the flag signallers display their feelings. After spending the last twenty-four hours using their caution flags to warn drivers of emergencies, they can now, literally, throw

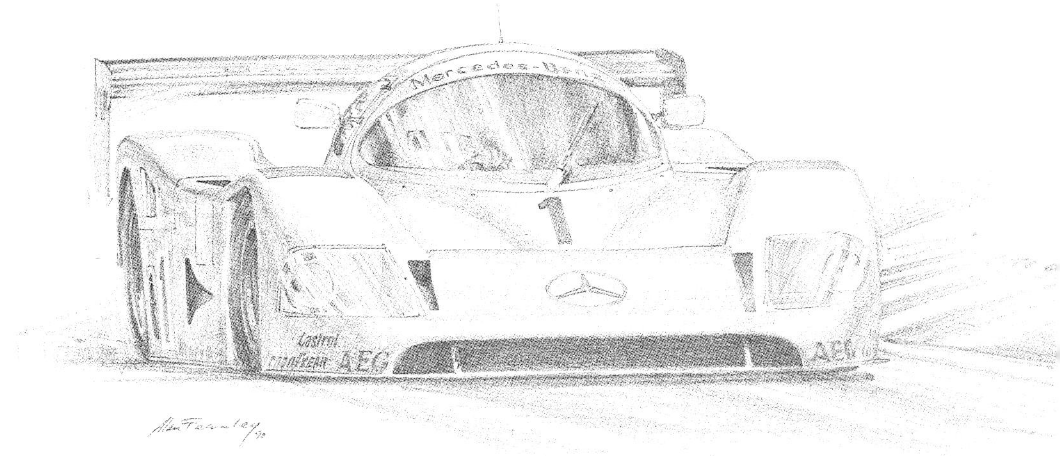

caution to the winds and in another Le Mans tradition give the drivers a colourful display of bunting.

Yellow flags warn of an obstruction on the track, yellow and red stripes, oil, blue means another competitor is close behind. The travel-stained, winning Silver Arrow covered 391 laps, a total of 3,272 miles, at 137.5 mph. It had thirty pit stops for refuelling and driver changes, and one unscheduled stop for the seemingly interminable repair to the undertray.

For the 1990 race, Mulsanne had bends inserted to slow the cars. Accordingly the winning car achieved only 359 laps, and the race average speed was cut to 126.8 mph. The international authorities were, they said, trying to make the race safer by reducing speeds on the murderous three mile straight. If the chicanes are retained, the 1989 race will go down in motor racing history as the fastest-ever Le Mans. Certainly 250 mph is among the fastest speeds ever recorded by any racing car - a tribute to the carefully-designed aerodynamics as well as the engine power and cool nerve required to achieve it.

THERE'S ONLY ONE WINNER: THE 1937 MONACO GRAND PRIX

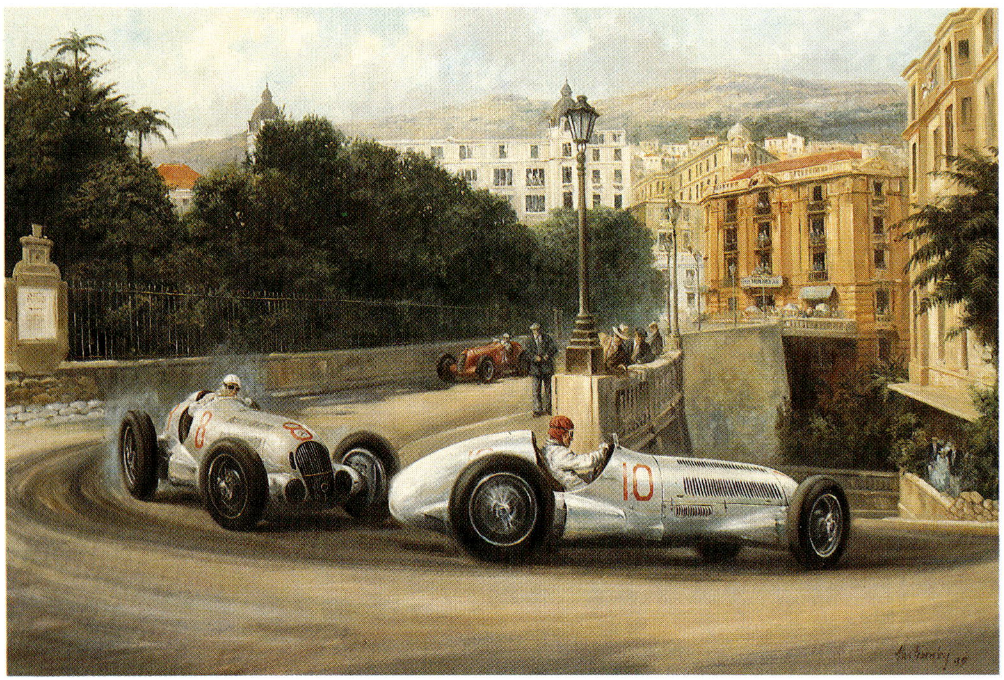

Von Brauchitsch on his way to winning in the Mercedes-Benz W125, after refusing to obey orders to allow his team-mate Carraciola through

Invoking the wrath of Alfred Neubauer, Mercedes' renowned team chief usually meant only one thing - dismissal. The glory of being invited to drive for the greatest motor racing team in the world was matched only by the ignominy of being dropped from it. Drivers disobeyed instructions at their peril.

Yet winning was the thing, and one occasion when Neubauer had to turn a blind eye to wilfulness was in 1937, at the Monaco Grand Prix. Manfred von Brauchitsch was a fast and brave driver but though his career spanned many of the great races in which Mercedes-Benz took part between 1934 and 1939 he was known as *Pechvogel*, the unlucky bird, and by Monaco he was resolved that his fortunes should turn.

The race was on 8th August, late in a season when the 5.66 litre Mercedes-Benz W125 had only scored one victory, the German Grand Prix, against three won by the C-Type Auto Union V-16s. The German race had been Von Brauchitsch's best result for some time, when he took second place behind Caracciola.

At Monaco he started alongside Caracciola on the front row of the grid, in cars with such a comprehensive spread of power and torque that they could if necessary, be driven all round the tight hairpinned track without changing gear. Monaco suited von Brauchitsch's driving style, he felt at home here, and he fairly threw the big car into the fray, cornering in a series of spectacular power-slides which contrasted with the measured style of Caracciola.

After their only real rival, the popular Bernd Rosemeyer (Auto Union) retired with steering failure, it became not so much a matter of a Mercedes victory as which driver would score it. The custom was that if one team driver was winning, another team driver did not harrass him, but von Brauchitsch, setting a new lap record, caught up on Caracciola and did just that.

Neubauer waved a flag to stop him; the usually orderly mechanics gesticulated agitatedly when the pair passed the pits side by side. Von Brauchitsch responded by putting his tongue out. The pressure brought Caracciola into the pits to change plugs, and even though he exercised his *droit de signeur* and caught up again, Brauchitsch drove the race of his life to claim his most famous victory.

The race average speed exceeded the previous lap record by the astonishing margin of over 3 mph, taking it to over 100kph for the first time. The record set by Caracciola in pursuit of his colleague stood for 18 years.

The celebrations went on well into the small hours. Mercedes held a victory dinner, after which the two rivals did one final lap of the track - by horsedrawn cab.

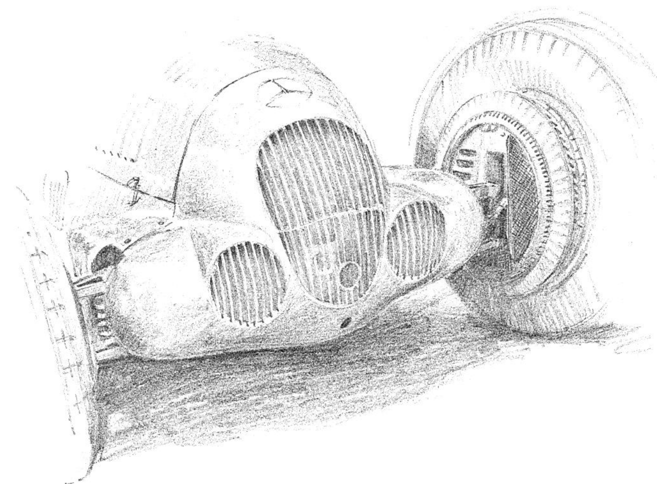

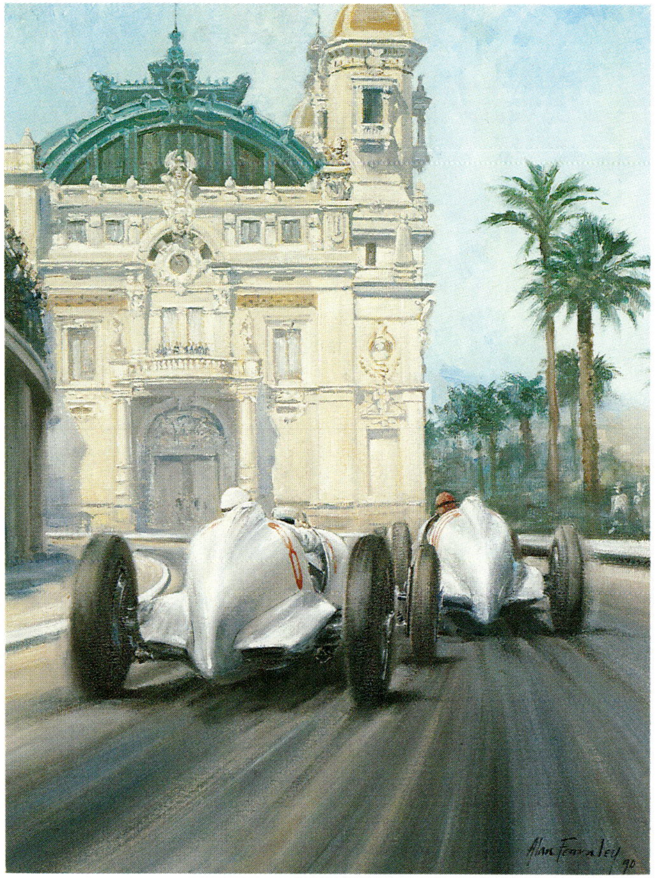

MONACO 1937

In Alan Fearnley's other painting of Caracciola and von Brauchitsch in the 1937 Monaco Grand Prix, they are approaching Casino Square. Ahead is the wedding-cake architecture of the famous Casino, overlooking them, spectators crowd the terrace before the Hotel de Paris. The action is caught from a viewpoint no camera could reach.

Monaco's famous hotel overlooks the square, through which the racing cars pass before plunging downhill towards the station hairpin. In 1937 the Paris Lyons Mediterranean Railway still brought summer visitors to the Principality. Fearnley chose the sharp left-handed corner to depict the cars nose to tail in the picture on page 28.

In both he captures the *fin de siecle* backdrop perfectly, the ochre stucco, and the ornate buildings many of which have been replaced by modern tower blocks. The Hotel de Paris remains intact, and hosts an annual exhibition of Alan Fearnley paintings.

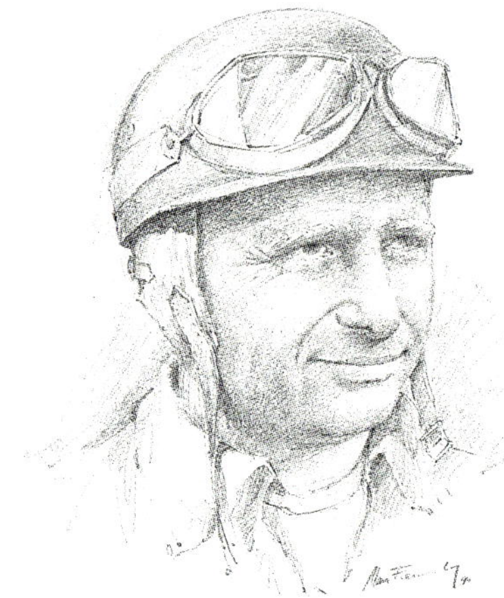

Above: Von Brauchitsch and Caracciola enter Casino Square at Monte Carlo during their famous duel in 1937

Centre: Juan Manuel Fangio heads off a Ferrari challenge in the blistering heat of Buenos Aires in 1955

Right: the Mass / Schlesser Sauber-Mercedes leads a rival Jaguar through Donington's curves in the 1989 Group C race

ARGENTINA 1955

The legendary Juan Manuel Fangio drove for Mercedes-Benz in 1954 and 1955. The technically advanced W196 had a 3 litre straight-eight engine, desmodromic valves which closed without using valve springs, and provision for four wheel drive to transmit the 290 horse power of which it was capable.

The 1955 season began on January 6th, at the Buenos Aires Autodrome, in the middle of a South American heatwave. The shade temperature soared to 37° C, ground temperature to 57°. The 96 lap race lasted three hours and drivers were forced to stop and let someone else take over while they recuperated in the pits. One of the Ferraris had five drivers. Only Fangio and a fellow Argentinian, Roberto Mieres, lasted the distance, Fangio winning at an average speed of 75.1 mph.

Alan Fearnley's painting shows how dangerously close the crowd was allowed to come to the racing cars.

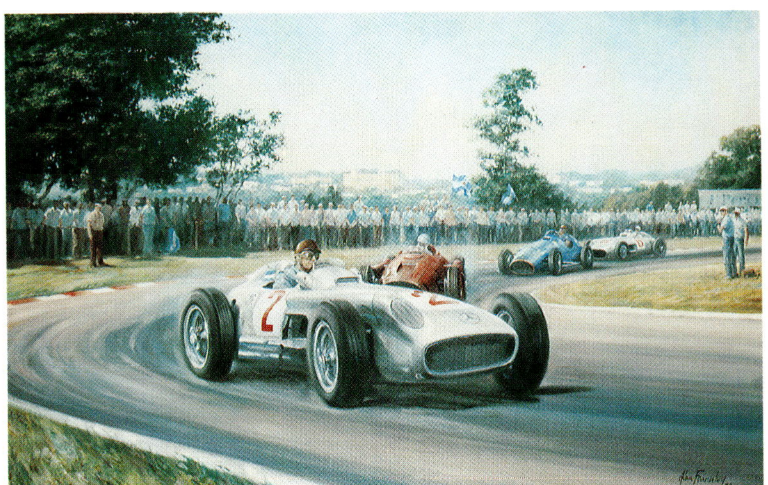

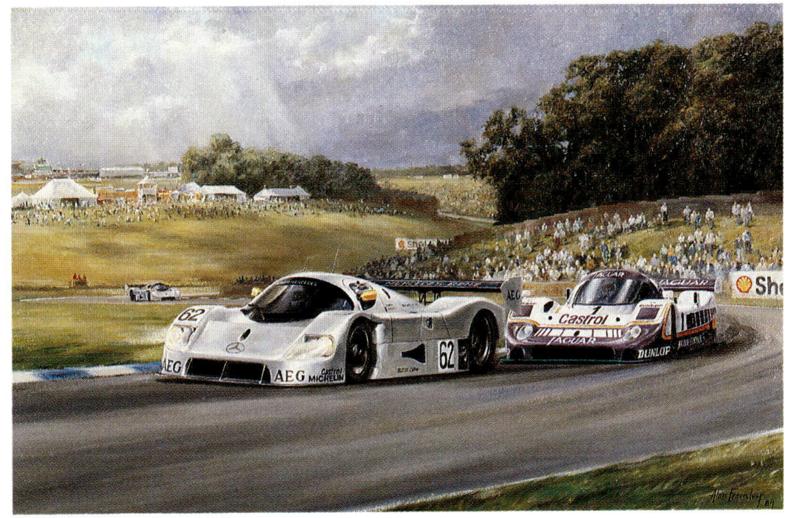

DONINGTON 1989

No modern endurance race was more keenly contested than when the Mercedes-Benz team returned to the sweeping curves and rolling hills of Donington after an absence of 51 years.

On their previous visits in 1937 and 1938, the adversary had been Auto Union, and Mercedes had lost both times. In September 1989, the rival was Jaguar on the 2.5 mile course which recreated the classic track of the 1930s.

At stake was more than a motor race. The long-distance championship of the world hung within Mercedes' grasp, and following its Le Mans victory and a convincing series of wins, the team started favourites. After 300 miles and three hours gruelling racing, the Sauber-Mercedes C9-88 of Jean-Louis Schlesser and Jochen Mass won from the similar car of Mauro Baldi and Kenny Acheson. The victory clinched the championship, and took Schlesser closer to his goal of the world endurance title.

REMARQUES

Frontispiece *W196 MERCEDES-BENZ: introduced in 1954 with full-width streamlined bodywork, the W196 later became an open-wheeled single seater.*

14 *1914 GRAND PRIX MERCEDES: the three-pointed star on the prow of the winning car did not yet have the laurel garland, acquired following the amalgamation with Benz in 1926.*

15 *MAX SAILER: the hare of 1914, Sailer won the difficult 1921 Coppa Florio for Mercedes and became racing department director in 1935.*

20 *W165: the shapely tail of the Tripoli car whose 1,492cc V-8 engine produced an astonishing 258 horse power at 8,000rpm.*

21 *ALFRED NEUBAUER (left): team manager from 1934 to 1939, and again during the post-war return to racing in 1954-55, Naubauer epitomised motor racing generalship.*

21 *HERRMAN LANG (left of group): Lang might have won a world championship of drivers in 1939, and was one of the few to return successfully to racing after the war.*

21 *RUDOLPH CARACCIOLA (centre of group): every generation produces a select band of drivers whose performances surpass those of their rivals. Caracciola's mastery in the wet became a legend.*

21 *MANFRED VON BRAUCHITSCH (right): born into a German military family, the red-helmeted aristocrat raced forever in the shadow of his brilliant team-mates Caracciola and Lang.*

24 *1989 SAUBER-MERCEDES: the 1989 cars are identifiable by the holes which lead cooling air to the front brakes on either side of the main air intake.*

26 *LE MANS, THE PITS: Alan Fearnley sketches the car with the front bodywork removed in order to get the feel of the structure.*

27 *JOCHEN MASS (left), STANLEY DICKENS (centre), MANUEL REUTER (right), : The winning drivers in 1989.*

29 *1990 SAUBER-MERCEDES: a second Le Mans proved elusive, but the 1990 cars won at Suzuka, Monza, Spa, Dijon, the Nürburgring, Donington Montreal and Mexico to win the World Sports-Prototype Championship.*

31 *1937 W125: used for racing for only one year, the voluptuous 8 cylinder, 646 horse power W125 gave Mercedes-Benz drivers twenty-seven trips to the winner's rostrum.*

32 *JUAN MANUEL FANGIO: generally regarded as the greatest driver ever, Fangio won two of his five world championships at the wheel of Mercedes-Benz racing cars.*

Printed by J. Looker Printers Ltd., Poole, Dorset.